THEORY OF PREPOSITIONS

The Crowded Circle, translated by Keith Waldrop
Le Collet de Buffle, Edinburgh, 1973

Reversal, translated by Keith Waldrop
Hellcoal Press/Brown University, Providence, 1973

Até, translated by Keith Waldrop
Blue Guitar Books, Plymouth
& Imprint Editions, Hong-Kong, 1981

Até, translated by Gary G. Gach
Minerva's Typorium, San Francisco, 1984

"The Maternal Drape" or The Restitution
translated by Charles Bernstein
Awede, Vermont, 1985

The Notion of Obstacle, translated by Keith Waldrop
Awede, Vermont, 1985

Objects Contain the Infinite, translated by Keith Waldrop
Awede, Vermont, 1995

A Descriptive Method, translated by Keith Waldrop
The Post Apollo Press, Sausalito, 1995

i.e., translated by Keith Waldrop
Burning Deck, Providence, 1995

The Right Wall of the Heart Effaced
translated by Keith Waldrop
Duration Press, Sausalito, 1999

CLAUDE ROYET-JOURNOUD

Theory of Prepositions

translated by
KEITH WALDROP

LA PRESSE 2006
IOWA CITY & PARIS

Published in the United States by La Presse, an imprint of Fence Books

La Presse/Fence Books are distributed by University Presses of New England.
www.upne.com
www.lapressepoetry.com

Library of Congress Cataloguing in Publication Data
Royet-Journoud, Claude, 1941—
Translated from the French by Keith Waldrop
Theory of Prepositions/Claude Royet-Journoud
p.   cm.

ISBN 978-0-9771064-1-7
1. French poetry. 2. Poetry. 3. Contemporary translation.

Library of Congress Control Number: 2005935122

First Edition
10 9 8 7 6 5 4 3 2 1

Each of the sequences in this book was first published
by Jean Daive in the review FIN (Galerie Pierre Brullé).

Contents

LLAN

the tools belong in an abstract realm

to avoid blows
he has made up his mind
the voices no longer couple

argumentation needs
signs in print
recovered ground
figure from behind

spit-gobs in semi-circle

after this I looked, and behold

A CLEAR SENSE

dazzle
faced with the nature of the crime
a simulacrum depletes the soil

Having chosen the angle, photographs the muscle. The image comes down. We're outside. Submitting and fallen. The voice holds the back up. An irremediable geographical confusion. She does not realize how close to her this world is. She only knows she treads over a dark viscous terror. A list of infinitives prolongs the accident.

on the floor
alphabet with ancestor

is it a lake
this free-lance eye?

the body slips in there
from a word to demolish

constrains the beast
to shift about and about

the numeral is to the left of the construction
they loom up
in restless movement
for space they have lightness

repetition is moving back
from the visible brink

the voice conceals
a state of weightlessness

she cannot interrupt its flight

around this stain
the day of the numeral, of the strangulation
the wrist burns the old way
name poised on the lips
they come together

"A language they have not thought in." A childhood quenched in the ruckus. She no longer improvises. (No offering, hardly a stir.) She situates the knife-edge, unsteadies the wound. The center of the room a cloth of linen. He locks in loss, forces childhood down and bears the image to its term. Framed stealthily, the landscape merges with the eye.

Like an unappeasable rage. Each blow reinvigorates
him. The fall gauges the distance gone. Fragility of
a sense "containing four simple bodies." Without
recognizing them, she takes up with them again.
Only the numeral resists. Sends her back to her
mine.

BIRTH OF THE PREPOSITION

ANTECEDENT

they are at war with the human

attention sagging
words should be put at an angle

a mirror calligraphy
is part of this penury

•

it's the dismemberment of a territory

the fall of an object
disorients the line

she reconstructs in the cold
a tale of skins on display

behind us
the animal is an erasure

pressing a finger on the wound
riles up verticality

sleep *in profile*

it falls to him to locate
buildups and breakdowns

reconciliations have taken place
no more space for the drama
or for crimes peculiar to a thought
the ancestor takes revenge
one last time

between them
innocence of a back

death weighed
tigers step into the image
a sentence is what comes to a stop
a savagery on the bare ground

objects make a circle around him
as if
the shift were deduced from this canceled body
the observer throws off all discrimination
force of amazement
in the mouth a sentence fills the world
loss of a vowel disjoints the sense
he tears them up with an improper usage

CONSEQUENT

encroachment of the name
counteracts perspective

the numeral legible underneath

by distancing sense
the portrait is finished

animality and disorder

to open to slash to scour

head placed on a cloth

no setting

—————————

it appears for no reason
making no claim on the simulacra
nor on its suffering

———————————

On the low table, an abstract approach to the world. He feels the
impression, the swiftness of percussed syllables. A breath frees
the lower limbs from their sockets. She no longer holds back her
strength. She calls reality to witness. The scene's proprieties foil an
intrusion from without.

*One color before the fall. Four circles arranged vertically. She
attributes the narrative progress to the storm.

———————————

I no longer distinguish angles
several beginnings come with the hand

cardboard as base

the consonants are distributed along the sides
and inside the building

water is an ink barely colored
a yes that carries and does not look back

on the accident

———————————

phrases circled
the eyes lose their grip
through with the obsession

before this one
erasure displaces accent

———————————

accounts with bite
butt against a closed world

color attenuates the drama

        having recourse to submission
to exhaustion
of an alphabet

(body in its prolongation)

———————————

The eye inverts proportions. A back seems to emerge from the penumbra. She taps the muscle. The vocal interruption is definitive. Her anger, a sleep that cannot be postponed.

––––––––––––––––––

judicial combat
animal postures avert the pain

––––––––––––––––––

each his own affair

a succession of bodies
whose identity disperses sight

nudity of the rough sketch
vocabulary of rioting seized by history
he sorts the acts
then regroups them

which begets a scene

TONE-DEAF

the border is a display of sense
a stretching of the voice

"from one side the flesh or the bones or the hand"

two full seas one after the other
lateral arrangement of derelicts

INFINITE BY ADDITION

taken up with the linen
she registers that as periodic behavior

two words (flung) divide objects
the image formed without being seen

He rejects the event and its simulacrum. The eyelid is naked, immodest almost. *Imperceptible and inseparable,* the other side of the hand remains in the dark.

after a semblance of pursuit
he abandons the territory

the details may be localised

◆

an arrangement of postures
gives birth on the verso
to various parts that accompany
the movement of bodies into sleep

the border is construed
alongside the image
not interrupting its fall

Revolving light. A line, from the chalk. Tongue
shielded from the world. Enumeration remains in
the mouth.

Between the walls of the heart and the heart, light
isolates the palm. Apart from naming. Reversed
letter. Anybody's history's covered up. The storm
carries off what's left. She displays her hand: an
hereditary tremor. To her I commit the quenched
body of a voice. Under the barbarian tongue, dried
ink. Under the barbarian tongue, unaltered.

scattered about the image
an unusual architecture envelops the child

he cries out figures
a bit of earth is displaced
it's merely the close of a day

one sees horses dragging part of a body in pieces

a sentence
relegates animality to other usages

repetition's end
placement of object makes more difference
than the object
it closes on the tongue
under the eyelid's hubbub
in the fatigue the eyes perceive
led forever astray

Bodies have suffered incisions that the image
does not retain. Air penetrates, inserts the word. I
yield without defining number, maternal basis for
achievement.

in case of a relapse
(a manner of) ruffling the *sky*

laceration or burial
the pack finds its victim

the living and his torso buried there

the arrangement of elements can endanger
the neighborhood
scars give no measure

the generation is in the sentence
stands apart from the muscle

OF NEIGHBORHOOD AND OF FORM

1.   I went into the image mutilated

2.   one brushes aside what the hand retrieves

3.   constraint of passage

4.   vocalisation

5.   as if he were leaving his body

6.   the pack springs from the point
in the world's bend and square
lost lip
"that child is my father"

7. *lamp whose periods of light, called flashing, are significantly shorter than its dark periods, called eclipses*

8. consolidation of the intelligible
this word we open in sleep
first and foremost, inert adjective color

9. she saves the stroke, gives it a framework
a word that confines the voice
aims at the back

10. the body reads from left to right

   on the board, shaky language
   this comes from outside
   knees bent and, here, fatigue

11. in the implicit ordering of gesture, of history
desire does not end with the mouth
it proceeds in another flesh
a ceramic heart shifts the motive

12.   three things sideline and primary
       some faces observed by way of conversation
       a body's intonation seeks its margin

13.   this incoherent part sets its own stake
       name like distance
       each element contributes to the fear

14.   voice suspended in childhood
       "till tomorrow!"
       incomprehension holds the space live
       "mirror image"

15.   temple, fist, hip, ankle

16.   safe from eviction, she gives way
       a question of dispossession
       insistance on snatching this term from other mouths

17.   I have watched you at the window growing

18.   before the leap
      a form is achieved

19.   square after square
      a little sense remaining in the palm of the hand

20.   *the number of the surface*

21.   they give the total architecture

22.   from the face on down

23.   *a particle of heart or of brain breaks off*

24.   the father's the end of the image
      he marries a mannequin and jumps out the window

SCENIC UNITY

WE WILL GO THERE, WHERE COMPASSION AND REGRET ARE DISPENSED

history is on his lips

BY MEANS OF A BODY

some photographs to promote cohesion

EACH ELEMENT IS SEPARABLE

in the deterioration of another body

BEHIND EACH SYLLABLE ENCUMBERING
THIS LINEN

an implement for concealing the entrance

USE OF A SENTENCE

"the dead take their pictures"

About the Author

One of France's most important post-'68 poets, Claude Royet-Journoud has devoted his life to poetry — to writing it, reading it, and disseminating it. He has edited several poetry journals, including *Siècle à mains* with Anne-Marie Albiach and Michel Couturier, *L'in-plano*, *ZUK*, and *Vendredi 13*. He also had a daily radio program, *Poésie ininterrompue*, which ran for four years on France-Culture, and was influential in developing public readings in France. With Emmanuel Hocquard, he edited two volumes of American experimental work in French translation titled *21 + 1* and *49 + 1*. His central four book sequence — *Le renversement*, *La notion d'obstacle*, *Les objets contiennent l'infini*, and *Les natures indivisibles*, all published by Gallimard — is now a classic in the long tradition of French poetic innovation going back to Villon. In it, Royet-Journoud brings an unprecedented tension and dynamic to the page and an insistence upon the materiality — the immanent reality — of the line as an act in space. Revealing the drama at the center of language, he places language at the center of our lives — as individuals, interlocutors, and cultures. Translated into 19 languages, his work has received many grants and awards, including the 2000 Grand prix de poésie de la ville de Paris. This new book focuses on the interstices of poetry, charging them with a vivid and compassionate force. Previously, it has been published serially in France in Jean Daive's review *FIN* and as a book in a Swedish translation.

This is the first title in the La Presse series
of contemporary French poetry in translation.
The cover image is the translator's typescript
with the author's holographic corrections.
The series is edited by Cole Swensen.
The book is set in Adobe Jenson and
was designed by Shari DeGraw.